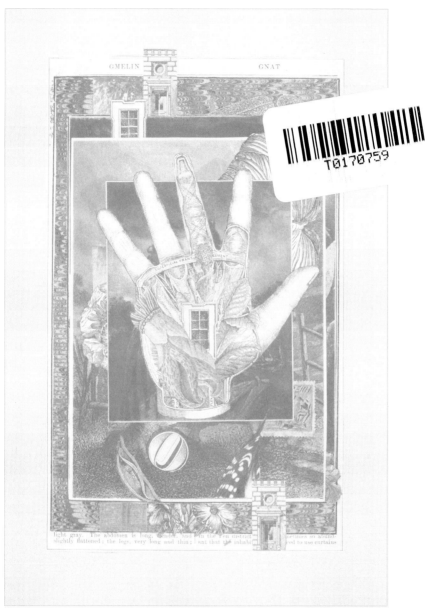

STIGMATA ERRATA ETCETERA

POETRY BY BILL KNOTT   **COLLAGES BY STAR BLACK**

ARTIST/POET COLLABORATION SERIES NUMBER THREE

saturnalia books

Saturnalia Books
13 E. Highland Ave.
2nd Floor
Philadelphia, PA 19118
info @ www.saturnaliabooks.com

ISBN 978-0-9754990-4-7

Book Design by Saturnalia Books

Printed in Canada by Westcan Printing.

Distributed by:
Small Press Distribution
1341 Seventh Street
Berkeley, CA 94710-1409
1-800-869-7553

The author gratefully acknowledges the following publications in which some of these poems first appeared: *Bat City Review*, *Dragonfire*, *Michigan Quarterly*, and *Tin House*.

Table of Contents

TITLES OF COLLAGES

INTRODUCTION

WHERE THERE WAS NOTHING, OR NOTHING MUCH, SOMETHING HAPPENS. We experience the world as a series of appearances, things coming into being. A truck rattles down the highway, a thunderhead towers over the fields. Where there was silence, something stirs in the leaves. The new appears; where there were eggs, there are now robins, where there were seeds, there are sunflowers. But the new originates in juxtaposition; the world rearranges the elements, throws things in our direction, assembles a new, unstable, momentary whole.

The artist participates in that work, or at least mirrors it, conjuring out of bits a shape, a structure, a form. This not-so-simple hat trick is marvelous in itself, but there's something especially compelling in a paradox of a poem like Bill Knott's "Total," which concerns the strange fact of its own coming apart:

Babel on the table falls,
my poem topples
into words
whose rubble shards

I try to stack back up until
they crumble still
again: but all
my efforts only pile

those collapsing tropes
in heaps
of worthless chips
which are

counted forth
with column patience
over and over
by the miser Silence.

I'd planned to stop after a stanza or two and comment on the poem's sly development, but I actually found it impossible to interrupt; the single-sentence structure won't let me, and neither will

those artfully enjambed stanza endings, which practically force one to keep going. Once you enter into the fierce little engine of this poem's progress, you can't escape, as the words go tumbling down the page toward the final, incontestable term.

But destruction, here, is a way of foregrounding creation. I can't help but imagine Knott building this poem out of the aligned, pleasingly related blocks of sound, following a train of sonic associations, from Babel to table to topple. If I isolate the words that follow that sonic pattern, a two-syllable rhyme on a clutch of trochaic words, the resultant list (Babel, table, topples, rubble, crumble) pretty much delineates the poem's arc. This suggests a line of thinking built out of sound, the poet's acute ear instituting then guiding a process of cognition in which music and meditation are inextricably intertwined. From the charged core of those words spin out the poem's ancillary sounds, complicating the pattern-making, setting off echoes of consonance and assonance and rhyme. We have here, in other words, an extremely artful poem about an unraveling, an accomplished portrayal of a poem not coming into being.

It comes as no surprise that a Knott poem should be a well-made thing indeed. I encountered his work first when I was seventeen or so, in Paul Carroll's anthology of young American poets, and soon I'd found a copy of the unforgettable *The Naomi Poems: Corpse and Beans*, which bore the signature of one St. Geraud, "a virgin and a suicide." Those poems were exactly what I wanted to be reading; the heady scent of a death-haunted, erotically charged longing came rising from the pages. I carried the book around with me until it fell apart. I wanted to write it myself, and I read myself into it so thoroughly that I felt, in some way, I had.

Knott's work has never lost its power to startle, and "Total" is a fine example. It represents a funny kind of creation. Where there was nothing, in this case, there is still nothing, but now there's a beautifully evoked and controlled text about the way whatever the poet intended fell to shards, leaving us, in its place, this, with its evocation of Silence as a fierce old miser directly out of Dickens, toting up those columns of words unspent. Column patience is a masterful coinage, instantaneously calling up ledgers and account books, spreadsheets in which assets are silently, meticulously, obsessively accounted.

Because this negation of a poem is a poem, it offers a world of local pleasures, signaling moments when form so seamlessly suits content that the two seem inseparable. First there's the rhyme, both inside the lines and sometimes at their endings. What begins as a regular pattern (falls/topples, then words/shards) tumbles in the next stanza into something else, four end-rhymes as the poet tries to stack up his troublesome terms. Stanza three tries to maintain that pat-

tern, but by the fourth line the project falls apart; tropes/heaps/chips gives way to the wan little are, as the tower of words goes tumbling down.

Knott's line-making is elegant; these small gestures mimic the work of the builder, stacking his word-blocks into a tabletop tower. Lines of sonic density (Babel on the table falls) make units of music and meaning that reward steady attention, but they alternate with others that seem transparent (in heaps), pointing to the instability of the project. A line like again: but all is a wonderful example of making much from limited means. That colon's the poem's dividing line, the midpoint between construction and dissolution, and in its way it encompasses a vision of the poet's work: again I try to make something whole, but all that happens is this little disaster. The colon glues those two parts of the line together with a firm suggestion of equivalency: to try again seems, inevitably, to the frustration and failure of but all…

Yet even this failure to bring order to things is enacted in firmly shaped quatrains, the old stanzaic form of narration, of confident motion in time. And it's the poem's rushing movement through its single sentence that sends us flying right back to the beginning, to understand where we've been, to marvel at how we got to this particular, precise zero, this nothing which is something indeed.

Knott builds out of fragments; he erases himself. How appropriate that these poems should be accompanied by a suite of collages, in which bits and pieces both make a new whole and remain, distinctly, bits and pieces. Star Black's evocative work here draws upon the vocabulary of surrealism, but like Knott himself she turns those strange juxtapositions and eruptions of dreaming to her own uses. Is there something inherently poetic about the collage? Like Max Ernst and Joseph Cornell — Black's spiritual forefathers — she places resonant, incongruous elements inside the framing rectangle and a new resonance occurs. That's exactly what poetry does, placing the found materials of language into a new frame that makes us see these words afresh, their light a little brighter, their dark edges revealed. Just as engravings are, words are bits of junk which carry fragments of culture and history, only their surfaces knowable. These two not-so-different sorts of creation together point back to the mystery of origins: the new arises, out of its polyglot beginnings, one unlikely thing rubbing up against another. Found things, assembled with the strange freshness of the ordering eye or ear, bring new and distinct presences into the world.

MARK DOTY

THE MOURNER

Cast in the shapes of his passing
he goes down ended avenues.
A lament-*passant*, he longs to
rub his ass antlers on statues

of Moonpie. He swans whether
he has a shelter where unfenced
with trees to testify its ground
the land around him is against.

And often he lets his face rain
above his mouth, above his eyes,
his nose: lets it hover in the mist
of its ignorant verities.

TOTAL

Babel on the table falls,
my poem topples
into words
whose rubble shards

I try to stack back up until
they crumble still
again: but all
my efforts only pile

those collapsing tropes
in heaps
of worthless chips
which are

counted forth
with column patience
over and over
by the miser Silence.

Commuter Skills Needed

I'm like a spaceship flooded with roadmaps:
The guidebooks that marked and led me here are
Archaic. All the ways they praise have lapsed.

They program mirage the moments I know—
Even my going home fails threshold then;
The path I nailed's a trail of blood whose flow

Is like what, a heritage halt, but just
How extinct can I get by existing,
Must I recant the past or can I trust

My family when they promise me some
Of us have not abandoned what crumbling
Almanachs applaud in words verbatim

From *Star Ache* reruns: they say our save screen
Is full of the old jism, the thumb-jam.
Can one yuckskull of us hold that vision

Safe, can they fly off fled inside its sky?
From vid to vid we lean, to wave goodbye.
It's like that thing that whatsit wrote, but I

Know it's mostly misquote. It don't apply.

ALOFT

once every student barber
to earn his certificate
would first have to lather
a balloon and shave it
then if it didn't burst
he passed his last worst test

but I wonder what happened
to that schooled balloon
did they use it again
or was it shown mercy
let go set free
to fly away safely

scrapeskin for a sheepskin
one nick will kill this bubble
let pupils skilled in scruple
cut its rubber stubble
here only dull shearers win
the hirsute-pursued laurel

a master's in mustache
a doctorate in down
Ph.D in peachfuzz
cap-strop-and-gown
more honors-blown diplomas
for tenured hands to slash

our blood stays bearded for
that educating puncture
light hearts inflate and then
learn one cut-throat lesson

to flunk is remedial
if pop-quiz pops us all

undrape look up and see
those balloons still floating over
our razor-grad degrees
they hang on the air
they dangle from a hair
no blade can sever

PAGEBOY

poetry is a matter of blond hair
of course dark works too you could use either

to wit tonsured sonnets and tanka conks
eclogue shags and song-of-bangs and blank hanks

add pastoral ponytails bob aubades
pomade odes and scads of other po-modes

brush them out bright for your any-anthol
dog-ear heads with the year's best doggerel

some word-gel helps if linebreak-curls won't hold
yet each poet fears her verse coiffure's bald

and the cowlick couplets the tress tercets
dread every stylist's editorial cuts

see formalist beehives and langpo buns
all cling together when the big comb comes

braid bards scalp skalds locklyric laureates
scared half their heaneys are a pollard yeats

let's tip our toupee to a topknot trope
before my permpoem flips its meter-mop

if the quicktrim rhythms they parnass-parse
today don't shampoo my poor metaphors

away I want to take and scan each strand
syllabic-chic and make it mane-enjambed

though most of the time I'd like to rhyme that
maybe-mussed-a-bit muse Erato's ringlet

ANOTHER FALSE EXECUTION

The crime-rate in our land is so great that
I could commit Murder A confident that
Simultaneously someone unknown to me
Would nearby be committing Murder B—

My plan's to confess to Murder B which should
Cover up my real guilt for A because if
I was busy perpetrating B how could
I have done A. The identical times of

The crimes and my evidentiary shame
Convince the law of that. The subsequent
Trial verdict shall hoistpetard my scheme,
Girding me with the gloat I'm innocent

Of that of which I stand condemned: I die
Endowed in the knowledge my sentence
Is wrong, thereby maintaining to the end
That moral superiority, that perfect high

Which is the cause of most crimes if not mine.

ALL OF THE WORDS

I know the days ahead
are the days I had given
up on before but when
were there ever any more.

Like waves that sleeve the sand
thoughts ruffle my forehead
until I must push driftwood
into facades of fortitude.

They sold their courage to gain
my fear. The fathers, I mean.

Time is thin in the arms of a machine.

Why are there more of us
waiting like this.
Eyelids mark the place
where sleep was always thinnest.

Even in the streets one is voiceless mute.
Listen. Wheels call by name
each passerby to blame.

What crybone schism, what night
is still trying to onsite
all of the words I ergo forgot.

NARCISSPOND

This pond saw someone once
But since then never none
Has ever another known

Imagine if your mirror
Lay cover buoyed by it
Recognition ink and pure

This water held no features
That were of us or any
Unless its blindness blurs

The eyes that see until they open
The face which is theirs only
In one ripple too many

Of course he says his name is
But all it is is just the same as

TOWERS

1.

Pisa's power to bend the head sideways
must be envied by history,
which can only force it forwards—
and Babel of course is praised
in every book (on every page)
for the way it slanticulates our words.

2.

Galileo drops a pound of lead
and a pound of feathers from the top,
one of which hits you on the head,
but which one—
(which head?)—
It makes you think, as well as stop.

3.

Every tower around here
is always in need of repair,
due to a superstitious habit
of leaning over
to peek into its 13th floor
to make sure it's still not there.

PASS AROUND THE COPIES

Have none of those nipples
left specks on my lips—
are there no stains on my fingers
from some of those warm hips?

(The ones I caressed
so far in the past
nary a trace must still exist.)

And what about the hands that coupled,
hands that cupped me—they
didn't deposit any spots?

Am I not a leopard
of love (a leper) covered
with its blotches stigmata errata
etcetera?

No: I'm not. Clean slate!
Bitemark, scratchmark, blooddrop—
none.

I'm blank, flawless, immaculate,
ready to be run
off on death's xerox, one

more poem perfect for Workshop.

NOVEMBERNEW

Scoldingly, the way a nurse
waves a thermometer at a corpse,
branches thrash above us.

I've read the instructions how
a compass should always go
consulted beneath a Maypole.

If space orientates with time alone,
our position fixed by Newton
may now be nearing Einstein.

Quickly I place a teakettle
atop a dead volcano
and learn to wait for its whistle.

North lost, the needle pierces my wrist.
The mist is in the forest.
Our sighs are in the farthest.

MYTHICAL RITUALS

Every day another roc moults,
every feather crushing
another town where
Notnose and Shyeye
and Wrongtongue
are conspiring.

As always the blood
of martyrs drips
straight to hell:
a purple plumb-line,
a Tyre-wire true.

The hundred-husked heartvalve
tries to find hope
in these instances.
But each day brings more.

Each day we open
a door whose keyhole
shrinks around us.

PLUNGE

at night one drop of rain
falls from each star
as if it were being lowered
on a string

and yet that storm of plummets
is never enough
to wet any of the planets
that pass through it

only the blackness the space
between us is washed
away by these singular
lettings-down of water

distance is washed away
all the worlds merge
for a liquid moment
our island eyes

and suddenly we understand
why umbrellas love
to dive
into clouds

SNOWS AND SNATCHES

Hurry while heaven's favorite
paperweight descends to press
the verses down that long to lift
us off within an endless draft,
away before their story ends.

Go bind in blind that white sheet-write
or let its stray-sleet countercloud
stay the fables that come to light
unfastening their thrust on. There

are no drifts a man of it might
survive until he melts every less
word that seams our pupilpane in
streams dividing day's span with
what its windownight withstands.

Now dawn strands his snows and
snatches in fall from all he's lost
unless that book once caught his
page wedged in both its hands.

POEM

barbershop in the desert
where I shave
the cacti daily
so carefully that no
pearl of their water
is spilled by my razor

come closingtime
the needles I've sheared
cover the floor so
I sweep them all
into the closet
to fructify the feet
of my secret cactus
which I keep
to replace the barberpole
who defected
up into the hills
out into the aisles
of my clientele

my virility my male
principle I'll
trim so bare
and never a drop
of its sperm
will I spare

WHAT

I envision a doctor saying
to me someday soon
(and any day is too soon)
your diagnosis
is terminal . . . then
I imagine myself
replying
well I've had a good life—

That daydream ends,
and I sit in my room
surveying, estimating
trying to guess
while I still can
what's good
about it.

Post

the one skull I'll never find
between my teeth is mine

anyone else's skull I may
(the dystopians all say)

have to suck the brains
out of if no food remains

postnuke postplague
(I'll crack it like an egg)

WISHINGWELL

I weigh the coin in my hand
against the water's clarity
that shines up at my shadow—
what wealth to smash apart that
gleaming calm with my claim
on the future, my need to be
rewarded with all I owe.
I stand above the well wondering
whether such a small as this
sacrifice is worth one wish—
the water is cold and stony
to a depth I can only guess.
And even if it reaches that far,
plummeting through the rich
rings of its sinking to reach
a bottomlessness whose core
is death-perhaps' deepest ore,
there where the end gathers
will my silver ever bring me
any of the gold it shatters?

The I Did

One memory from childhood
how when it was summer and hot
at ground level where I stood
above me I saw the tops of trees
palpitating in a proper breeze

that never came down to ease me.
I can't say I swan why I remember
what it is that makes it linger or
else enriches such a significant
nor could I see it now if I went

on a breathless day and looked up
I would not be far enough away
physically for the contrast: memory
needs that distance for its truth
to swerve from the present's path.

Is it right to hold the past fixed in
former attitudes like tops of trees
or whatever it is records history's
external focus switched to days
depictions drawn by winds upon

clouds or branches flexing wide
their leisure of purpose pause
from the hell of here. Sight cannot
even in summer when it is hot
share the air enjoyed by the eyed.

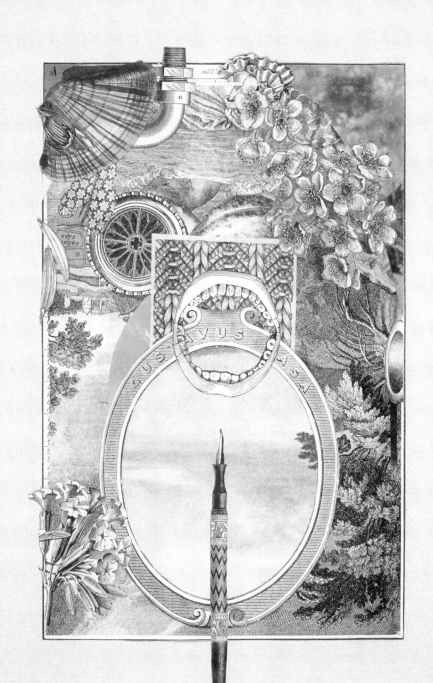

RECONCILIATIONS

To be married while sleepwalking
and wake up on your honeymoon
abandoned by the prankster pals who
led you both in blind steps through
the nuptial rites that culminate here
in what-the-hell: to wake with lewd
glowing rings glued to your fingers,
the hotel bed unmade around you—

Outside your bridal suite what resort
explodes with ennui, its white tropical
walls will yield that one photograph
that shows you shining, your eyes
aimed shut by the sun. Natives wave
bandannas that flaunt their unstorebought
power. Your pockets pacified by beggars,
that day is almost over. The night awaits.

And then you're home again, but oh
it's so hard to restore the routines
that are a now of the old, the remote
control too big for two who hold hands,
noting how the pattern of the crimes
seems to shift from channel to channel,
but always that financier has fled
the country, has found his freedom where

you lost yours. Soon in the freezer section
fate may feed your fingertips, or taking
out the trash becomes an expedition:
for the accomplished somnambulist
escape is easy everywhere. But even
that land whose lack of extradition
has followed you throughout this farce
will fail to exile the happy couple.

SNUFFED

The candle's leaf
is what we call those drops
that cling solidified
up along its length
after it's been blown out—

We switch on the overheads. Outside,
branches bode, bode, bode.
What
do they predict?

Descent is all,
they're not specific, unlike
our phrase
for this froze ooze
(which beads the bole)
(and which is more like sap than leaf)
this effluvium, this sheaf
that trickled from a flame we lit once
days or years ago.

Time, our sentence, is specific.
Memory, its syntax, vague.
The melt is where they meet—
inksoil syllables dribbling down a page.

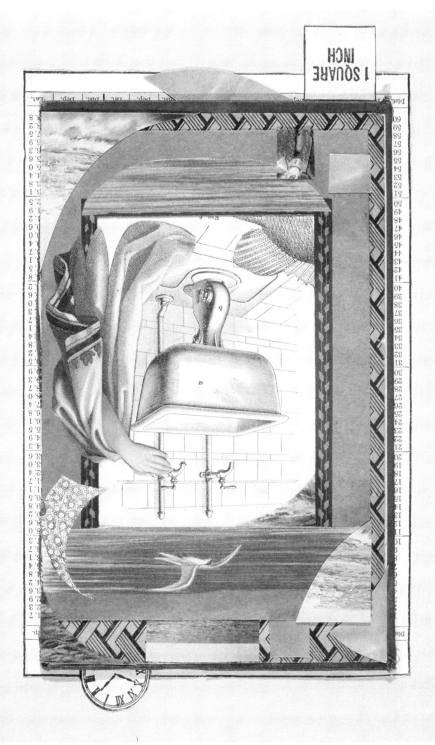

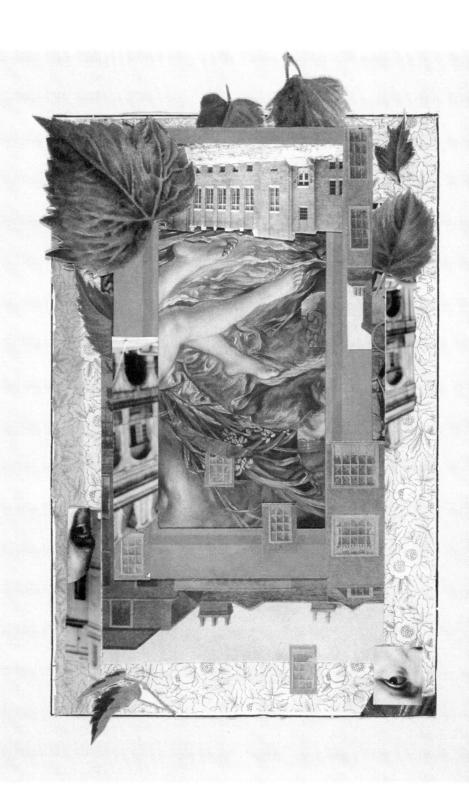

THE DAY AFTER MY FATHER'S DEATH

It's too complex to explain
but I was already in
the orphanage when dad died
and so that day when I cried
to keep the other children safe
from my infectious grief
they left me in lockdown
in some office where I found
piles of comicbooks hid
which they had confiscated
from us kids through the years
and so through wiped tears
I pored quickly knowing
this was a one-time thing
this quarantine would soon end
I'd never see them again
I'd regret each missed issue
or worse than that I knew
that if the day ever came
when I could obtain them
gee I'd be too old to read
them then I'd be him dad.

An Instructor's Dream

Many decades after graduation
the students sneak back onto
the school-grounds at night
and within the pane-lit windows
catch me their teacher at the desk
or blackboard cradling a chalk:
someone has erased their youth,
and as they crouch closer to see
more it grows darker and quieter
than they have known in their lives,
the lesson never learned surrounds
them; why have they come? Is
there any more to memorize now
at the end than there was then—
What is it they peer at through shades
of time to hear, X times X repeated,
my vain efforts to corner a room's
snickers? Do they mock me? Forever?
Out there my past has risen in
the eyes of all my former pupils but
I wonder if behind them others
younger and younger stretch away
to a day whose dawn will never
ring its end, its commencement bell.

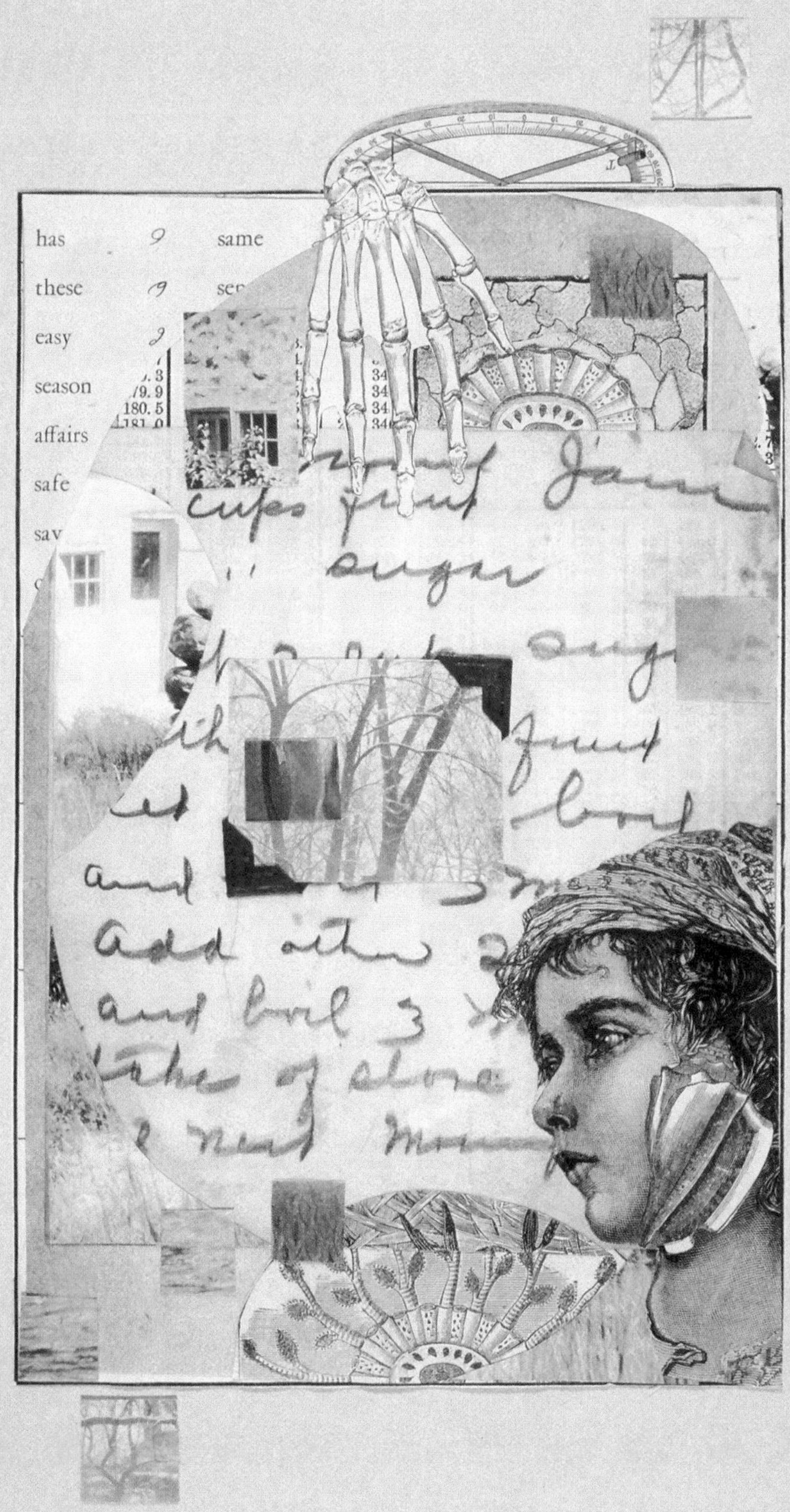

has   9   same

these   9   sen

easy   2

season   79.9
                180.5

affairs

safe

sav

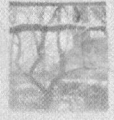

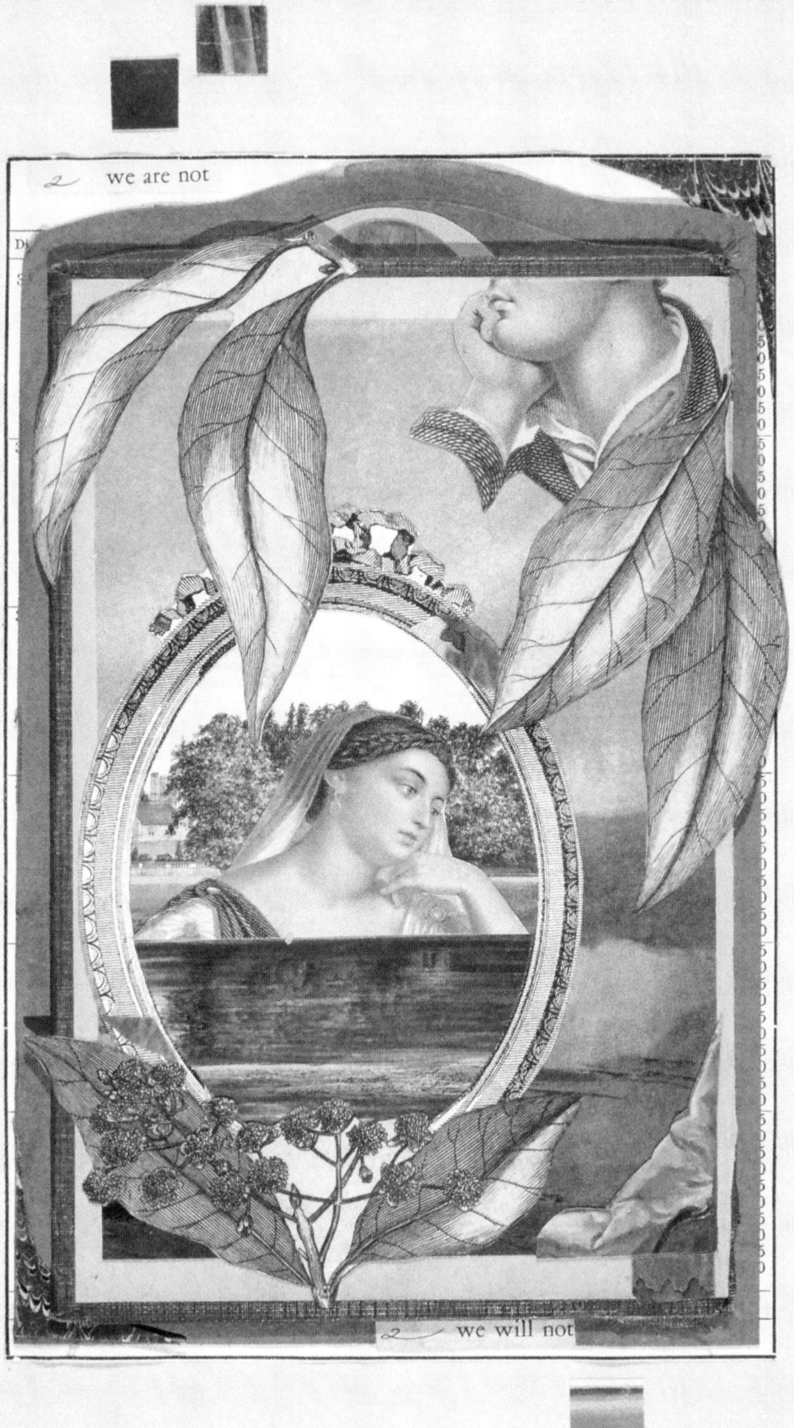

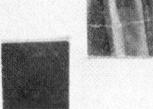

we are not

we will not

WAIT TILL TONIGHT

Sometimes a dream will show me
the words I need to begin and end and
then take them away and leave just one
word or, like last night, three or four:
"the arms of care." That's all. There
were lots more but they vanished when
my eyes opened; they were of course
the words I need here now to justify
this. How can I forgive myself for
forgetting them, forgetting that which
might have made me whole for a while
holding you all in my arms of care?

REFLECTION

Some are afraid of the deep;
me, of the shallows.

It's not possible to drown in it,
but it is possible to delve in it;
which is worse?

I lean over a mudpuddle,
bend to a pane-drop.

The shallows
is where I sight myself;
the abyss
shows all you others.

Which is worse?

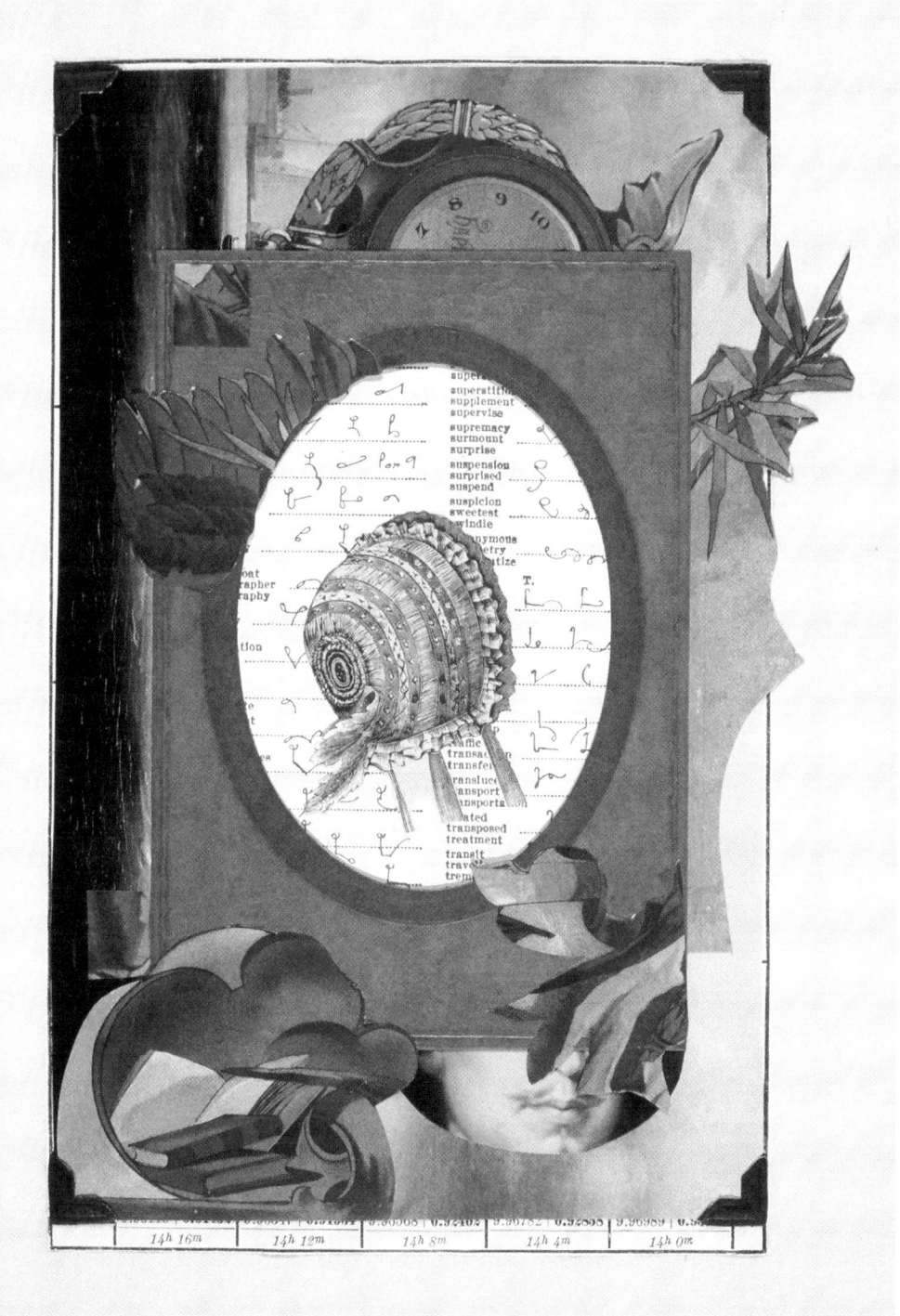

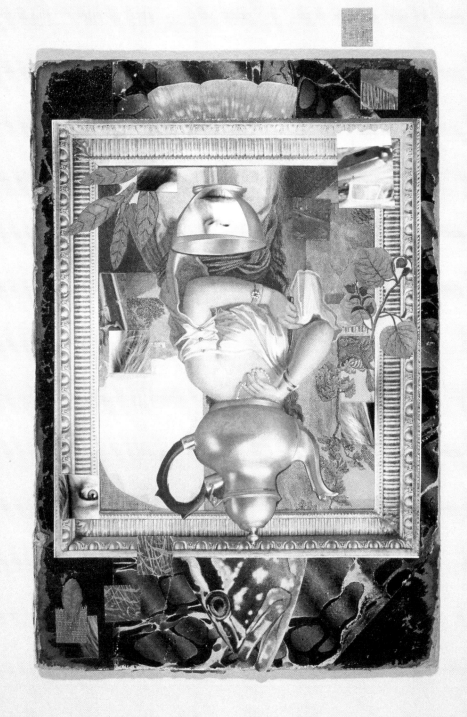

DISCRIMINATION

Although not lab-test verified,
I would guess that the pages of porno
magazines turn yellow and crumble
from the sperm shot onto them
faster than the poems in my books
turn yellow and crumble from
the saliva spat at them by readers—
or is it a fallacy on my part to assume
that the products of love are always
more acidic, more corrosive
than the products of loathing?

ENCOUNTER

Is there truly no secret
I may forget for you?
No, you answer, others have already
forgotten all my secrets for me, thank you.
You're polite about it.
A shrug says sorry.
Those others, they are obviously your true companions,
whereas I—
Now you go back intent on what you were doing,
before my insane interruption.
I crackle my cigarette pack.
I look at you sideways.
I don't want to intrude, I'm discrete.
I sit and drink my cappuccino. Will we ever meet?
I doubt it and besides,
I've already forgotten what it was
I bothered you with in the first place.
Whatever it was I said,
it's your secret now.
I'll never know.

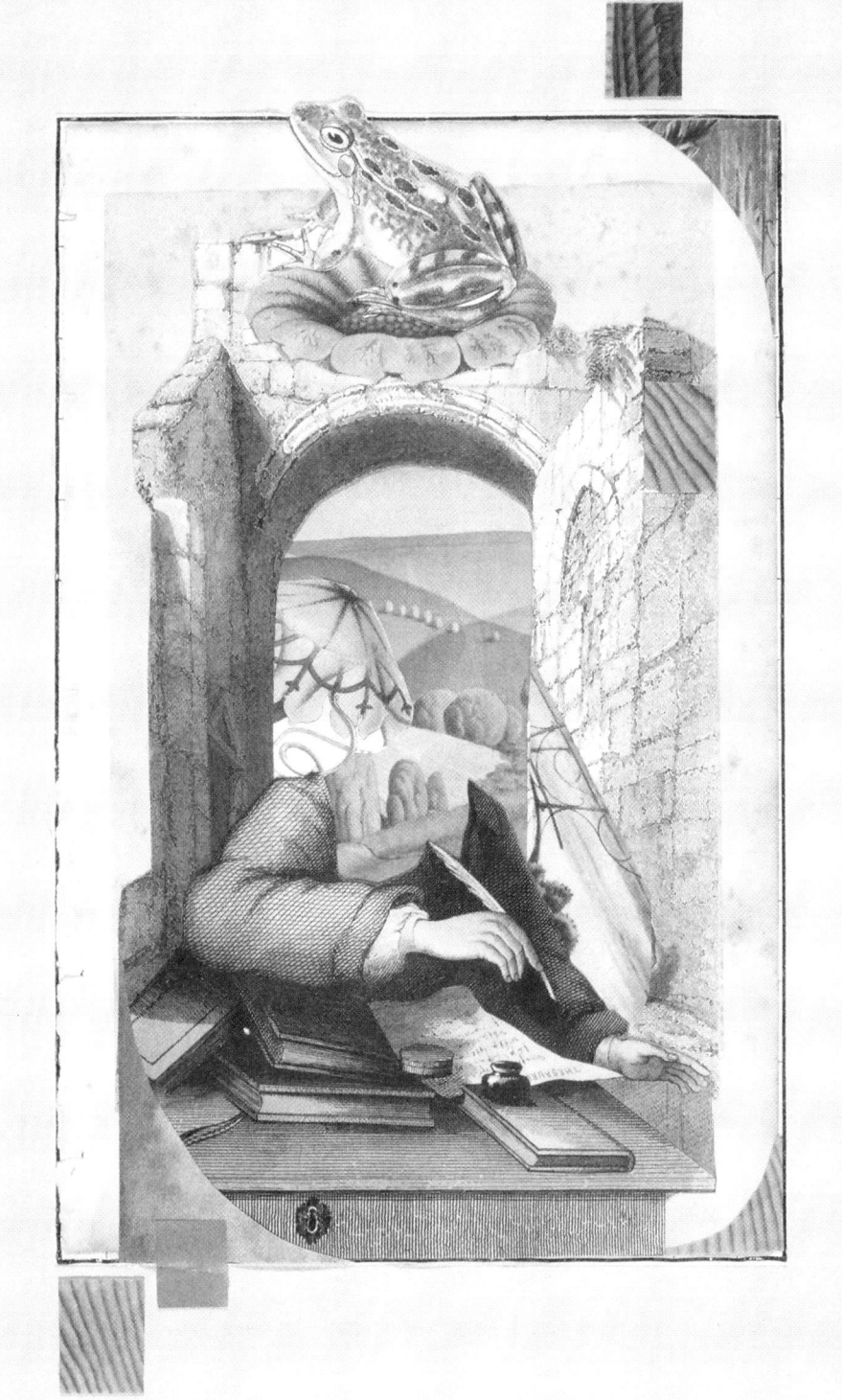

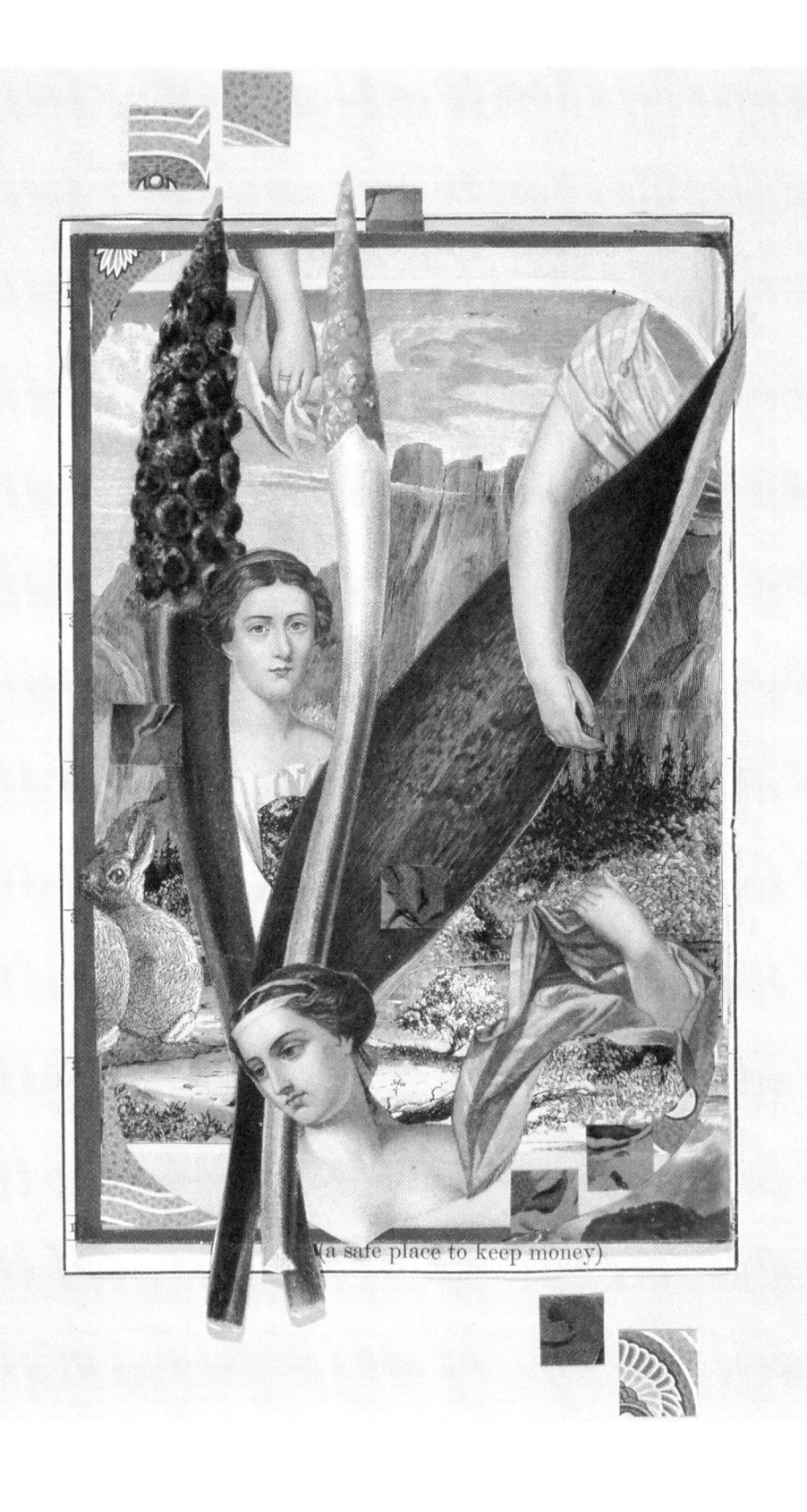

(a safe place to keep money)

EVICTION PROCESS

Wreckball all the highrises:
then use the cornerstones of those
leveled towers to create my castle:
composed solely of foundationstones,
each one of which was blessed
with a ceremony, a literal
groundbreaking and therefore whole;
each block unique,
inscribed with ritual aggrandizements;
each planted solemnly:
each underpin-laid as the bedrock
its lesser brothers would rest on:
use only these rootstones to raise
the walls of my eyrie house hideaway
whose forbidding frame will have
no real infrastructure, whose form
will be a spiritual suspension
(cradle crux kernel hub core)
wherein each establishingstone
must cohere solid with the weight
of its having once been named
in salutation as such—but surely
when these maidenstones these
consecratalstones are placed
together to make home my dream
my ideal occupancy, then surely
due to the baseless act
of imagining this acme of architecture
I will not be allowed to live here.

An Understanding Unnaturally Prolonged

Someone was talking on the telephone
marked for hello while at the opposite
end of the café the phone for goodbye
was free: we couldn't hear her voice at
our equidistant midway table crowded
with standup toasts shouted down, our
congrats visible in the confidence with
which napkins surged from loose collars:
at the booth across from us sat a party
crying, shaking their faces out of their hair.
They stayed our share with such contrast—
hours went by, days; we feasted, they
lamented. On our exit finally we went
past the hello phone still in use, she was
still talking there and we were amused,
amazed at her persistence until, peering
way down toward the goodbye phone
still on its hook, suddenly we understood
the boothful who wept in our wake. How
we continue in hello though there is none
to go goodbye. How we live while they die.
And as we did we were often struck by
how long that understanding took to pass,
yes, how unnaturally it seemed to linger.

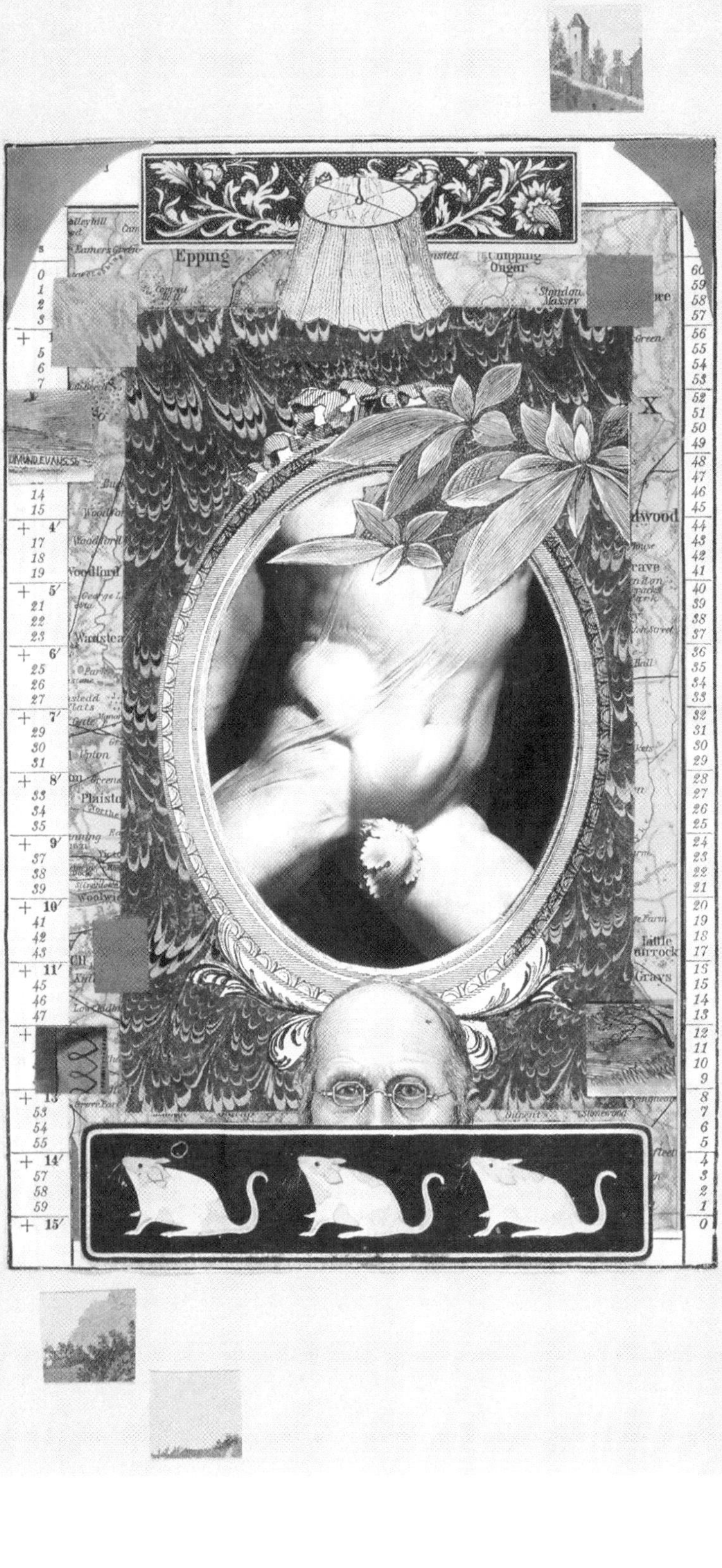
Epping
Chipping Ongar
Woodford
Grays

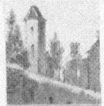

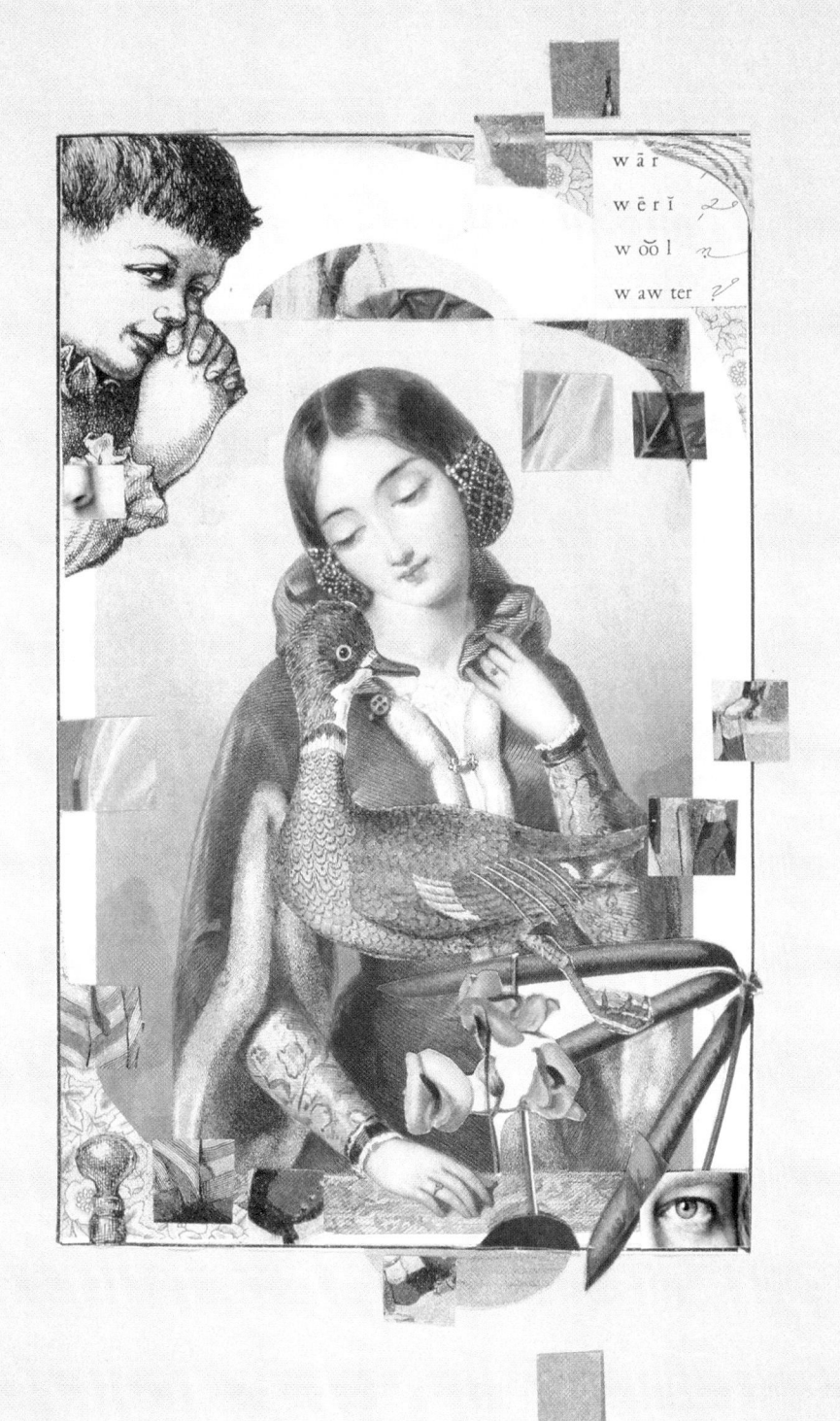

wār
wĕrĭ
wŏŏl
w aw ter

INTENT

Stalactites can hang their mangy lava
anywhere, but I have to cling to these arms
that descend into hands. Nights I probe

the walls for guidance to the cave
they're hiding in there. Ordinary house
on any street with huge divestitures

of hope above it, the soul I was saving
for capture. And so I have to adhere
to this doorless expanse scattering birds

its bareness. This sky is why I cannot pry
myself loose from certain caresses I gave
years ago; their tentacle strands leave

ampukisses on limp horizons. These
tendernesses dispensed in my wake
constantly plant tendrils around my intent.

THE SILO

The silo
longs to feel itself full,
if only for an interval—

Its ribs expand once yearly as
the host of harvest
enters a space
unbearable to the nil,
painfully utopian in its display
of plenty.

But soon after that sate
moment slowly
each ear of corn is paid out
over the days until
only empty shucks
and echoes fill the crib-cage,
its grasp lies
reduced to wisps, to waste.

Mice round the slats of its walls
without pausing because
nothing's there
on the floor. Nothing and all
of nothing's needs.
Modest winds brush through.

Circumspect as someone
retracing their signature
on a death certificate,
going over each letter
a second, unnecessary time.

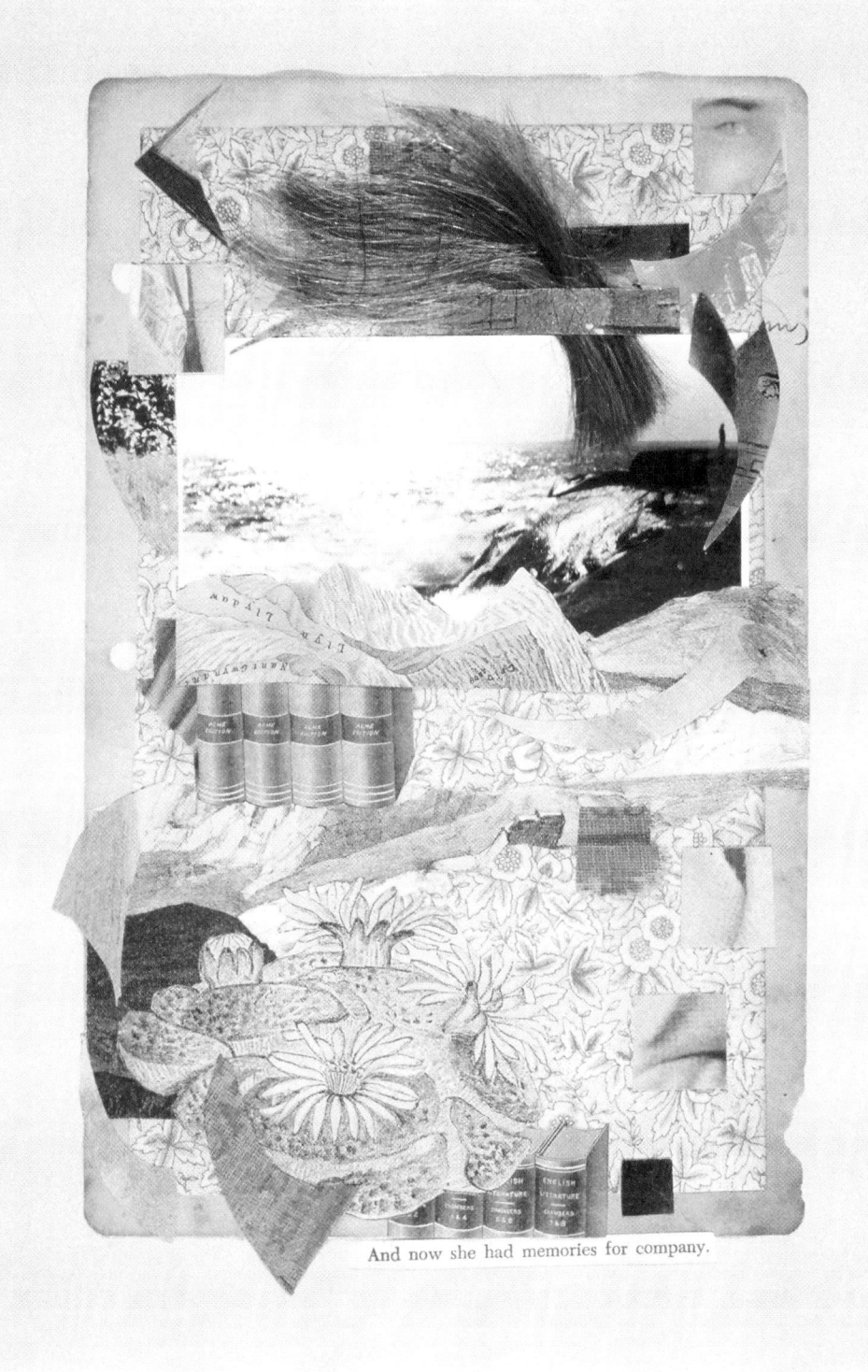

And now she had memories for company.

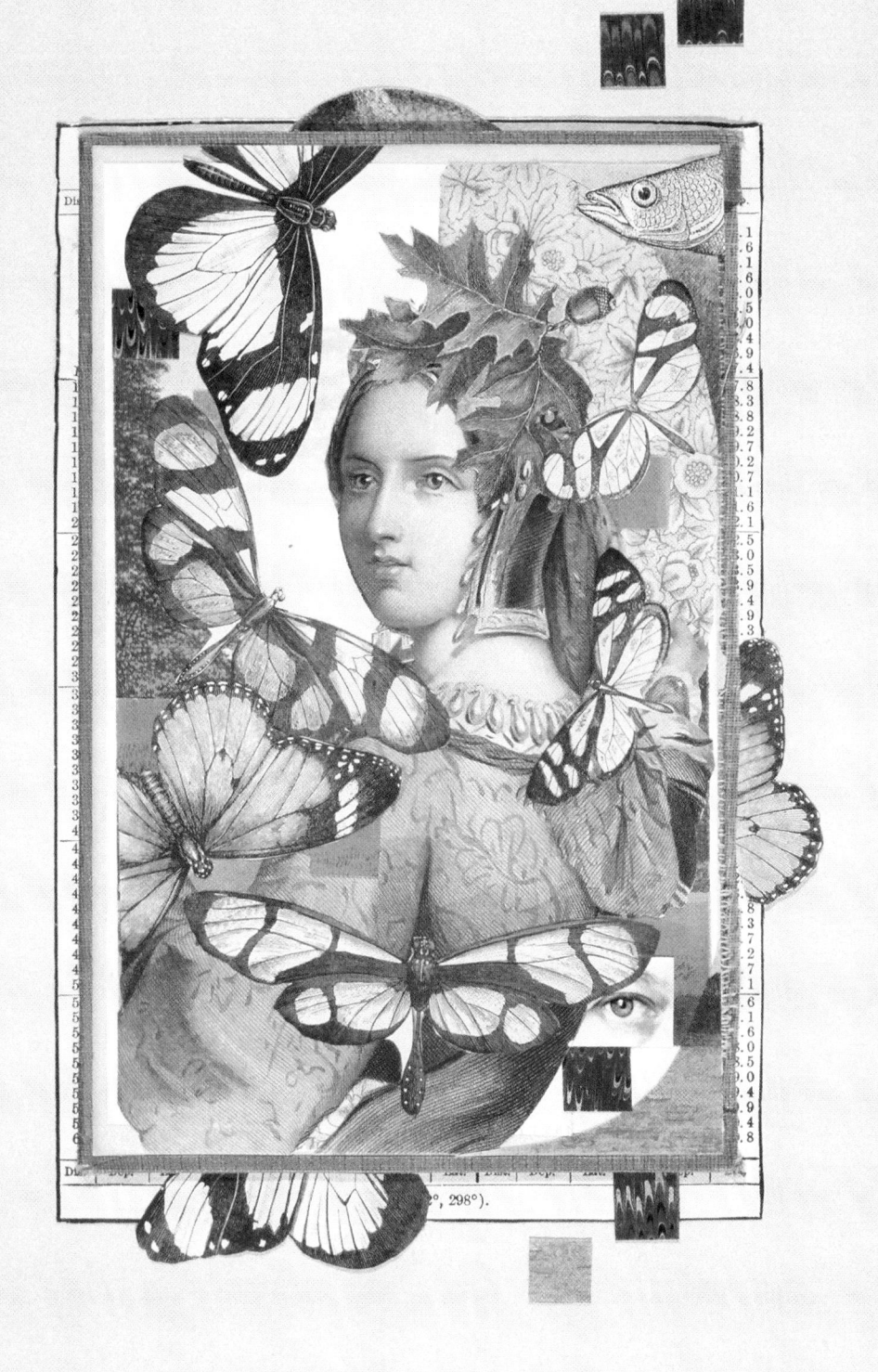

°, 298°).

PANE PERHAPS

I bear the bulb that never burns out
so why do I change it daily, discarding
every light as if it were dark—is this
how I try to extinguish doubt? If
all the face I hold to its lips outshines
and shapes each path my steps ape:
fills each millisecond socket with
such purpose that the stray-goer gaunt
with desire for that glow no other
mirror gyred into my eye can descry
finds himself most of lost, most of past—
resentful he soars toward that mirage.
By now his staircase is replaceless in
this house of spiral pursuant maze,
told to a secret code deciphered by
coincidence but aren't they all: in rooms
where our waits wilt like the heart
of a coffee-vend machine dripping
time, moments for an hourglass where
intonations of high tide trip one's tongue.

Day the sky takes up its task of wings,
night the way we lay down ours.

Epitaphs

Their meaning seems to be there aren't
enough of them: why else would "REST
IN PEACE" show up so endlessly doled
from gravestone to gravestone, "LOVING
FATHER, DEVOTED SON", "FAITHFUL
SPOUSE" and all the other ubiquitudes—
every cemetery's a clone of its own one.

This sameness betrays a bewildering faith
in the inadequacy of words—it implies that
whatever you or I might choose to have
indited there for a final phrase of grave
would be as lacking and even less would
fail to qualify as equal to these primeful,
these small, one-sign-suits-all sentiments.

But the main reason may simply be size:
maybe these commonquotes total right
and totemize the most to measure down
our lives, they make as much meat as one
can carve on a standard tomb, they sate
whatever else the eye fills up with after all.
Maybe these filigree graffiti fit the bill.

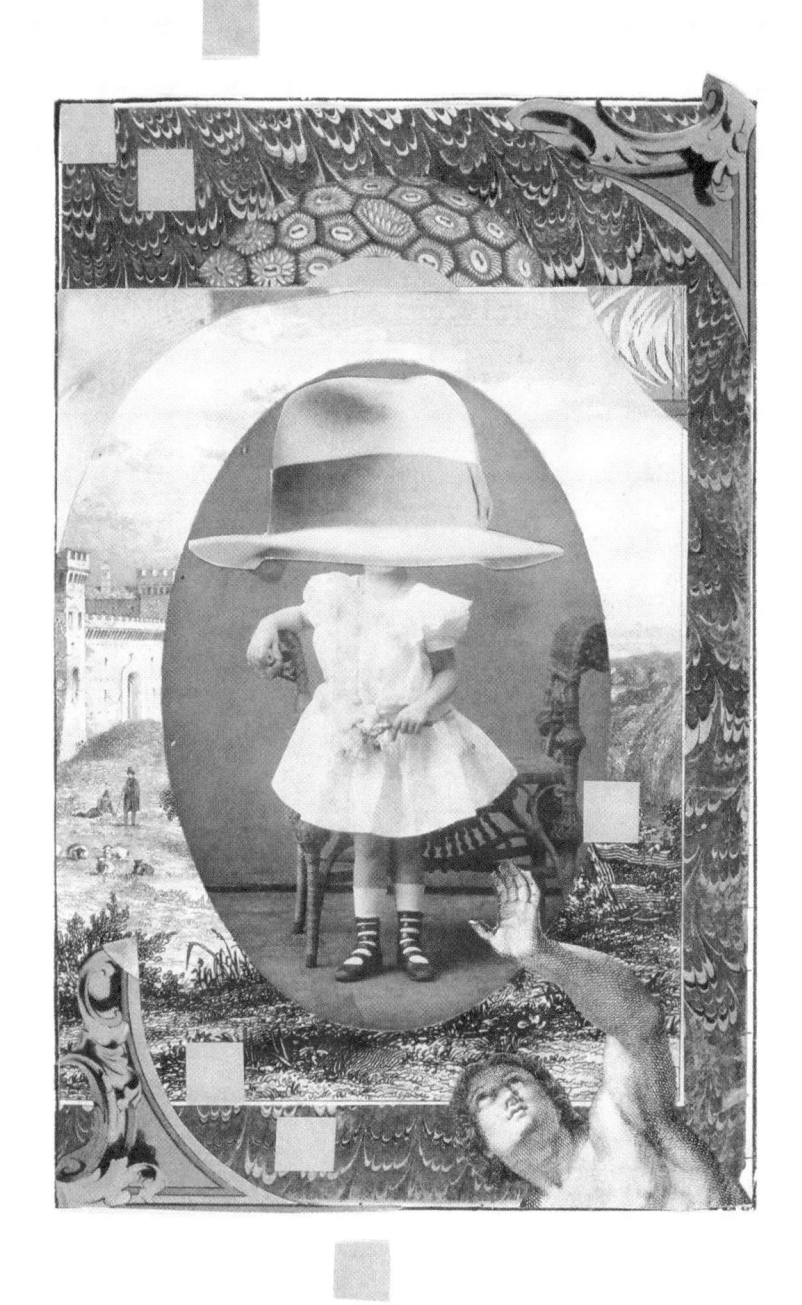

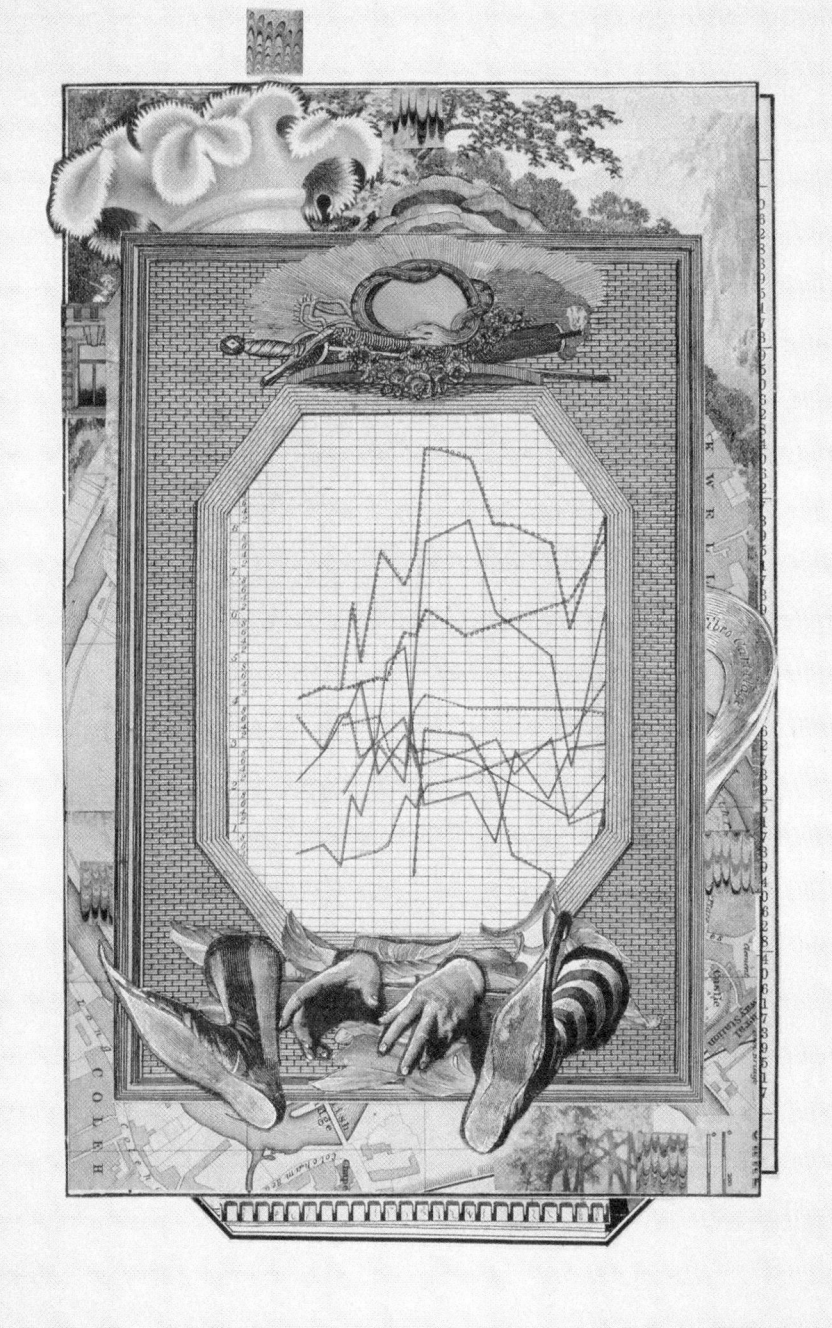

AGAIN

One of my pores creaks
when I pass through it,
as I invariably do—

if I found that aperture
whose verge protests
at my constant

farings forth,
I could oil it with
kisses or apologies,

promises to restore
the tender sill its
welcome mat violates;

to renew the world
it opens onto, to destroy
the one it opens into,

if I only knew
why it alone
amongst the millions

dares to complain,
to voice its distress
in the form of flesh

when I pass through
as I invariably do,
soon for the last time.

THE ONE

If gravity's angel is
the unfallen one,
the only one
aloft, if.

It's paper I write on, page
you read, but is it ever
papge? That
unpronounceable

is where
the sacrifice
occurs, the merge—
Like Sylvia in Leopardi's lament

we fall, in fact we flop:
our slack hands helpfully point
out the inadvertent
directions of death—

the right a tomb in the air,
the left a mausolith,
the one I write with.
And now all

others recto verso show
their distance the one,
the only one
I live with, if.

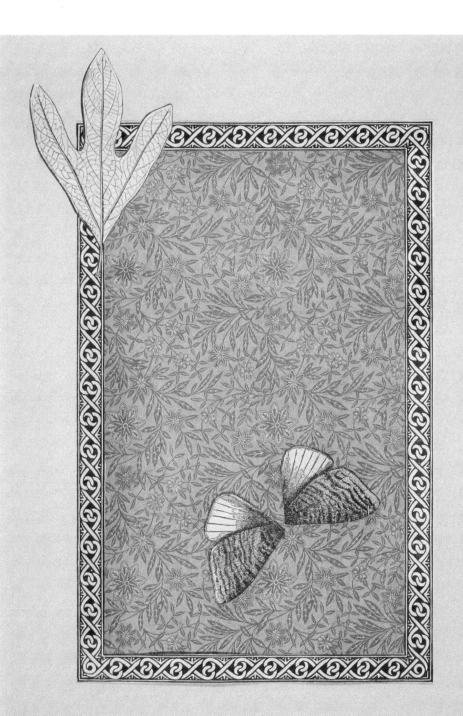

ADHESIVE VALENTINE

not knowing where you are
not knowing who
so I'll coat with glue
all the envelopes I mail

where most words fail
mine will still pursue
kept in these veils of glaze
every postal maze

no matter how far
no matter how overdue
they will find the true

letter bound for you
and there be pressed
adherent to its address

APRIL AFTERNOON

From barberpoles the white
should be stripped to bandage
all the bypassers' wounds.

Their clothing seems to consist
of tickets brandished to the theater;
every kiosk's counter is bare.

These shapes are assumed
out of fidelity to the mask
that covers them with less and less.

And yet there is always the danger
of excess. Naked, the street
might lie prey to a merchant's

deliberating broom: birds
and categorical pushcarts might tie
cherrystems to our eyelashes.

Spring imposes its pomp, its priorities.
In the middle of this effortless palace
an orgy takes off its socks.

AIM

I have arrived but
Have I, have I really—

Maybe to say that I
Have arrived is wrong.

Maybe I have instead
Merely uncovered,

Bared for myself
A destination that

Was here all along,
Till now concealed,

Till now not found.

(—But have I really gone?)

OEDIPUS RIDDLED (HEPTASYLLABICS)

the course of his crime unfolds
each time at a blind crossroads
whose four legs forever show
less murderous ways to go
but every young man must opt
to stand his ground and stay stopped
so to prove unmoved he waits
daily till he demonstrates
to the empty thoroughfare
how brave how bold how strong there
beneath noon's knelled prophecies
bound to meet all enemies
on his own two feet alone
or has he halted hearing
the stepsound of his unknown
father's cane tap tap nearing

PROOF

If time is relative,
so that it might be 12 AM
in 1966 for me,
12 PM in 3002 for you,
and for everyone else
another when-ever;
and if each person exists
within this own moment,
then, since there can exist only
one true time, one of us
is alone on this earth.

It's theirs by right,
because theirs is the exact present
and ours isn't.
The rest of us are like nowhere.

Imagine the rest of us
just haunting around,
pounding upon the walls of
that one person, pleading
with him or her
to please let us in, please,
but will they ever hear our cries.

Aging Into The Avantgarde

When the mirror paints itself,
how true to life
the results seem—
But when it paints others, well,
take me, I who have posed so long
my patience has earned
the most flattering
exactitude: so why
(as the years go by)
is there this blurring
appearing where my face is;
is expressionism occurring?

When it comes to its own
likeness, it's photorealism no less—
the mirror paints itself
perfectly, whereas
the one it does of me
(I can see now as I lean closer)
in the end turns out to be
nothing but a sort of art brut:
the brushstrokes grow
more fauve, more cobra
each time I look.

POEM: AS IF THE AT-TOUCH WERE SOUGHT

I know there is something lost
in the palm of my right hand,
and perhaps I shouldn't look
for it, but through weakness I do—
or is it duty drives me? Whatever
it is that has gone astray here
escapes me as I scrape and peer
at what seems so utter placid
insipid a place. Or is my vision
superficial:—hasn't this skin
struggled against the invasion
of interfering ulteriors—alien
hubristic objects—items—elements—
contents of any kind—: don't
its lines over-hint at the strain
it must have suffered to try and
maintain that emptiness, that
apparent void which stares back
as if to say, what I have least
misplaced there's me? Refusing
the fortunes which palmreaders
boast of, should the palm insist
on its innocence in this case,
indemnified against all loss—
(could any future who dared to
trespass here, bear that cost?)
Vacant, perfect, such purity
grows normal: what an ordinance
between my grasp and the poor
things I grasp!—albeit dollars, kisses
or others' hands, hands always
wishing they could unyield world's

toehold. For in whose cause would I
commit that sin and rip open,
vacate this veil that might conceal
every fate its surface traces
clearly as a false demure of lust—
already else, how can this lack
elusive mask occupy me wrist
downwards, and beyond that
unawares as it were, in thought
only, or has it covered most
of that too. And isn't this just what
the thumb is searching for (or
is it checking up on—testing
the smugness, the smug resilience
of such a consummate, ingrained
transparency) when, absentmindedly,
automatically, without finding
anything but that which is lost,
it rubs itself alongst the rest,
those strangers known as fingers?

REPLICA DAYS

A statue disguised
as the lines in your palm
longs to love you
though still you resist
its endless caresses.

Just as the smoke
of burnt portraits
clings to mirrors.
Similarly ashes of dolls fill up
a child's footprints.

Rain also, in the event
an iceberg's
mourning-clothes.

Dawn drapes you:
you put your arm in one sleeve
and the other sleeve
begins to bleed.

POEM

when the balloon bursts
where does all the air
that was inside go

is it bound together briefly
by the moisture
of the human mouth
that birthed it

poor pouch of breath
long expulsion of nothing you
must dissipate too
nor remain intact
no matter how pantingly
against the outer atmosphere
you might try to secure your
whoosh-hold

and what an effort
what heave and heft-work
what strain of frame what rib-rift
to have to lift to shift around
all that oof and uff

why strive and huff just
to stave off death
to survive
to be a substance a stuff

to live live as a pocket
a cluster
a cloud
to maintain your interior
mode

I can understand
that having once been
contained in buoyance
you'd want to retain
that rare coherence

you'd pray to stay a one
to remain a unity an
entity a whole in
this unencased heaven

but smatter of ghost
how can you persist
or save yourself
when all us others disperse

dissolve in draft
little whistlestuff
pathetic kisspuff
flimsiest flak

up into the sky goes
two lungs worth
of earth
unstrung
unloosed
the exhaled
soul of a boy a girl

alloonaloft
aloftalloon
lost

PERSPECTIVE

I must look down to see
the things that fall
into the well

(coins
teardrops
stopsigns

sunsets
planets
etcets)

because when I don't
look down to see
them suddenly

they all
start to fall
on me

TOGETHER OR APART AS OUR FAVORS CARRY US

someone to pause and take pills with
during the act of coitus
or the fact of cosmos

the days remain pain punctual
their numerals cracked exactly
at noon and night

they fall in a noise of wings
who's talking who's talking
each phonecall designer begs

where a sleep of engines calms
the horizon we go alone
to smoke our halo's last cigarette

in v's we leave we leave
wherever
our favors have carried us

Stigmata Errata Etcetera is the third of a series of collaborations between artists and poets for saturnalia books.

Stigmata Errata Etcetera was printed using the fonts Adobe Garamond Condensed

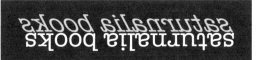

www.saturnaliabooks.com